Purgatory 101

by D.J. Cyprich

First published August 22, 2011
(Feast of the Coronation of Mary)

ISBN: 978-0-9880974-2-1
Version 3.0.3
Updated September 29, 2019

Table of Contents

Part 4: Prayers and Devotions

Part 5: Appendix

Free Book

Purgatory 101 is a free book and copywritten by D.J. Cyprich. It can be downloaded at

http://www.ecclesiabytes.com/free-stuff/purgatory-101/

If a digital or printed copy of this book was sold to you, and not obtained for free, you should ask immediately for a refund and let me know about the violators. I can be contacted by e-mail at dj@cyprich.com.

The e-book is available for free on Apple iBooks, Google Play Books, and Kobo. The Amazon version is $0.99 USD which is the minimum price they permit for e-books ($0.99 is the new free!).

Author Bio

D.J. Cyprich is a cradle Catholic who starting taking religion seriously at 14 years of age, was confirmed into Catholicism at 18, converted to Protestantism a few years later, then reverted to the Catholic Church about 3 years after that. He has remained in the Catholic Church since then and has developed a strong interest both in apologetics and helping the souls in Purgatory.

His time in the Protestant community was not wasted. It transformed him into a real, truth seeking Christian from a lukewarm, superstitious Catholic. Seeking the truth is what led him back to the Catholic Church.

One of the first things that he took an interest back in the Church was Purgatory. This was the result of a seed planted years earlier when he read the timeless classic, "Read Me or Rue It". This booklet had a greater effect on his life than he could imagine at that time. The result led to starting the Ecclesia Bytes web site which not only provides extensive information on Purgatory, but also on Catholic apologetics.

Introduction

This is not your typical book on Purgatory. There are many books in circulation that terrify their reader on this topic and leads them to devotions for the holy souls out of fear. They are taught that their suffering will be worse in Purgatory if they don't do more to help the holy souls. Over time, the fear dissipates and so do the devotions. What these books accomplish are short term results which the reader quickly forgets and then has little interest in the plight of the holy souls.

Purgatory 101 takes the approach that in order to truly help the holy souls, we need to have a clear understanding of who they are, why they are there, and what can be done for them. This understanding cannot be rooted in fear. It must come from a love for them as our brothers and sisters in Christ who are suffering and need our help. We help them because we want to and not from a scrupulous fear of punishment if we ignore them.

This book is a compilation of 13 years of articles on the Holy Souls Online web site. Content has been edited and added to make it more readable and suitable for an e-book. The wonderful thing about an e-book is that it can easily be updated without a costly print run. If you join the mailing list for this book, you will be kept informed of all updates to it.

It is my hope that after you finish reading Purgatory 101, you will remember the holy souls in a daily devotion and that you will do more for them than attend an All Souls Day mass once a year.

Part 1

The Main Doctrines

All these souls [in Purgatory] are greatly loved by Me. They are making retribution to My justice. It is in your power to bring them relief. Draw all the indulgences from the treasury of My Church and offer them on their behalf. Oh, if you only knew the torments they suffer.

Jesus to St. Faustina

Chapter 1
What is Purgatory?

Purgatory is a much misunderstood doctrine among Catholics. It is commonly believed that this place is a second chance to be saved, or that one can sin all they want and still be saved through its expiatory fires. Purgatory exists as a result of God's mercy. The requirements for entering Heaven are very high because **"nothing unclean will enter it"** (Revelation 21:27). To go directly to Heaven you must be completely free from the stain of sin. What this means is that you cannot have any unrepented venial sin in your life, you must have fully paid the penalty for all of your sins, and you cannot have attachments to the world that takes you away from God such as materialism, jealousy, and hatred. With this in mind you can see how difficult it is to avoid Purgatory, but with the grace of God it can be done.

The purpose of Purgatory is to *purge* us of all our unrepented sin, atone for all of the unexpiated sin in our life, and remove all worldliness from us so that we can fully love God and each other.Once the stain of sin has been completely removed, the blessed soul may enter glory and full communion with God in Heaven.

Where Is Purgatory?

Theologians have been debating for centuries on the location of Purgatory. Some of their conclusions are that it may be at the gates of Heaven, located in an area of Hell, or perhaps it doesn't physically exist at all but is simply a mental state of purification before entering Heaven. The fact is that no one really knows the answer to this question. The Church has not made any infallible declarations on this. All that we know is that it does exist and this is what has been taught since the Apostolic Age.

The purification process in Purgatory is painful. The holy souls see how their sins have separated them from God and deeply regret what they have done. Even venial sin causes suffering because although it is a minor sin, it does offend God since it is disobedience to His will. The holy souls have an intense desire to be in Heaven but are prevented entry because of their impurities. This causes great pain within them and they plead, **"out of the depths I cry to you, O Lord; Lord hear my voice! Let your ears be attentive to my supplication"** (Psalm 130:1, 2). Even though the souls suffer greatly, they also have a great joy within their hearts from the hope that one day they will be in Heaven. St. Catherine of Genoa said that *"apart from the happiness of the saints in heaven, I think there is no joy comparable to that of the souls in purgatory"*.

How to Help the Holy Souls

Prayers for the dead have been said since the Old Testament era. The Old Testament Jews believed that it was **"a holy and wholesome thought to pray for the dead, that they may be loosed from sins"**(2 Maccabees 12:46). Praying for the dead is one of the seven spiritual works of mercy.

There are many devotions you can do to help the holy souls. **The first and greatest act is offering Masses for them. This is the most powerful prayer we can participate in and if we only have one devotion to the holy souls, this should be it.** More souls are freed through the Mass than by any other prayer. Remember to pray for the holy souls during each Mass you attend.

The second most powerful prayer is the rosary. The repetitive simplicity of this devotion hides its greatness. After each decade, you can add the following prayer:

O my Jesus, forgive us our sins, save us from the fires of hell, and lead all souls to Heaven, especially those in most need of your mercy.

There are many things that you can do for the holy souls. The important thing is to do something, and do it consistently. Exercising just one day per week will do you little good, and praying infrequently for the holy souls will do them little good as well. Remember them every day and you will see the difference in your life as a result of their gratitude.

Chapter 2
Indulgences: Gifts for the Suffering Saints

Indulgences are just as misunderstood as the doctrine of Purgatory. This is a closely related doctrine and, like Purgatory, rejected by most of our Protestant brethren. Even Catholics today don't believe in indulgences mainly due to ignorance in what it is and prefer to believe that it's a relic of the past that was abolished by the modern Church. Of course, indulgences are still valid today and can be used to reduce your time in Purgatory.

The Protestant Reaction

The abuses of indulgences in the middle ages was a factor in the Protestant Reformers separation from the Catholic Church. The Church at various times sold indulgences to raise revenues. Pope Leo X (1513-1521) used the money from indulgences to construct St. Peter's Basilica in Rome. There were abuses from people like Friar Tetzel who claimed that *"a soul is released from purgatory and carried to heaven as soon as the money tinkles in the box"*. Martin Luther used things like this to justify his revolt against the Church.

In response to these issues, Cardinal Cajetan (1469-1534) condemned those preachers who were using indulgences for commercial gain and not following the true teachings of Christ. Also, the Council of Trent (1545-1564) provided Catholics with a teaching on indulgences and what to do when problems occurred. It commanded bishops to record all abuses *"and report them to the next provincial synod"* (Sess. 25, Decree on Indulgences).

A Parable

The doctrine of indulgences can be illustrated with a simple parable. A mischievous child was one day walking by the home of a man who treated him very badly, or so he thought. With his immature sense of justice, the child felt that he should punish the man by throwing a rock and breaking one of his windows. So he picked up a stone, hurled it, and watched with glee as it flew through the air and shattered the glass. As soon as he heard the glass breaking, he began to think that this probably was not the wisest thing to do. The enraged home owner who came running out of the house towards him felt the same way as well. The child, in an act of perfect contrition, begged for forgiveness. The man, being very merciful, accepted his forgiveness and promised not to tell his parents what he did, thus sparing the child another painful lesson in morality. But the man said that even though he forgave what he did, the little rugrat would still have to pay for the damage.

The Definition

When we sin and repent of our sin (*repentance means asking for forgiveness with the intent of not repeating the sin*), God will forgive us but we still have to pay for the damage we caused due to the sin. The damage is the "stain" on our souls when we sin. Even though we are forgiven, the stain remains.

It should be understood that sin produces two effects on our souls: **the debt of guilt and the debt of pain**. We are both guilty and deserve pain (or chastisement). When we repent of our sin, the guilt is removed but the pain remains. The souls in Purgatory do not have any stain of guilt, but they have the stain of pain which must be removed in order to enter Heaven.

An indulgence, therefore, is the remission of the penalty due to sin, or in other words, it is a "payment" to remove the stain of pain from our souls. The payment is not in a monetary sense because we cannot purchase our salvation, but it can be made through prayers, acts of charity, and acceptance of the suffering one endures throughout their lives.

Partial and Plenary Indulgences

There are two types of indulgences that we can receive: partial and plenary. A partial indulgence is the easiest one to obtain. It will remit a part of the penalty of the sins we have committed, while a plenary indulgence will remove **all** of the stains of sin in our soul.

In order to get a **partial indulgence**, we must have the intent of obtaining the indulgence, we must be in a state of grace (i.e. repent of all of our sins), and say the prayer or perform the act which would lead to an indulgence. We are permitted by the Church to get as many partial indulgences each day as we wish.

A **plenary indulgence** is more difficult to obtain. In addition to the conditions attached to a partial indulgence, we must go to Confession and receive Holy Communion. We must also pray for the intentions of the Pope, which include world peace, the growth of the Church, and conversion of non-Catholics. A plenary indulgence can be obtained only once per day but those who are in danger of dying may receive a second plenary indulgence in the same day.

Distributing Indulgences

There are two ways in how the indulgences can be used. We can apply them to pay for the sins we have committed, or we can give the indulgences to remit the penalty of sins for the souls in Purgatory. When we give our indulgences to the holy souls, it will shorten their stay in Purgatory, give them some comfort, and may release them from Purgatory if their soul is completely purified from the stains of sin.

A partial indulgence given to the poor souls in Purgatory will shorten their time there, while a plenary indulgence has the great grace of completely purifying the soul and allowing them to immediately entering Heaven. Unfortunately, in order to be granted a plenary indulgence, we must be completely free from the stain of sin which is difficult to do. But we should try anyways. If the indulgence is not granted, it will at least be partial and will provide some benefit for the souls.

It is a great act of charity and mercy to pray for the dead. The holy souls will not forget what we have done for them and they will repay us a thousand times over for all we do. May God have mercy on them and may we pray for them every day.

Chapter 3
Private Revelations

There are two types of revelation: general and private. **General revelations** are the teachings handed down to us from Jesus and the Apostles. These revelations ended with the Apostles and they must be believed by all Christians. **Private revelations**, on the other hand, have been occurring since the time of the Apostles. These are not new teachings to add to the Gospel. They are messages from God to help us in our lives, or to help others. They can also be warnings to problems which can be averted if we heed them.

Private revelations can be dangerous, such as the apparitions at Bayside which lead people away from the Church to a destructive sect. This is why the Church needs to examine each private revelation to determine if it's worthy of belief. The local bishop is in charge of examining the visionary and apparition before making a judgment on it.

When a private revelation is approved, it doesn't mean that everything that it teaches is true. It means that there is nothing in it that is contrary to faith and morals and they can be read without danger. Belief in it is also optional. You don't have to believe in the teachings of Our Lady at Fatima, but you miss out on a great deal of graces if you don't.

Every revelation on Purgatory is a private one. There are many frightening visions and also visions which inspire those who hear them. Caution needs to be exercised here because most visions have not be examined or approved by the Church. The traditional books on Purgatory use the tactic of scaring the reader to get them to help the holy souls, i.e. if you don't help them, you'll suffer a long stay in Purgatory. These sorts of tactics only work for a short period of time because eventually the fear that caused it is forgotten. Love and knowledge of the holy souls is a better way to bring about faithful devotion to them.

Use caution when studying private revelations. Study your Bible and your faith to help you discern them, and of course look to your bishop for the final judgment.

Chapter 4
The Gratitude of the Holy Souls

"If one knew what we may obtain from God by the intercession of the Holy Souls, they would not be so much abandoned." (Padre Pio)

If you want to make a great friend, do something extraordinary for them. Kindness is usually repayed many times over in return for charity. What do you think would happen if your prayers and sacrifices released a soul in Purgatory? This would be a soul who was suffering the pains of hell (due to separation from God) and then brought to heaven in full communion with our God. Their joy will be immense and they will remember you. In fact, they will be constantly interceding for you at Our Lord's feet for not only your salvation, but for your other prayer requests as well.

Praying for the holy souls has lead to miracles. If you have a seemingly impossible or very difficult problem to solve, help the holy souls. They will repay you many times over. Do you have problems that overwhelming you? These may be health, financial, or family related. Help the holy souls, offer masses for them, and encourage others to pray for them. The holy souls will pray for your needs and intercede to Our Lord for you.

Interceding for the suffering souls requires a sacrifice on our part. These are acts which greatly help them and, in turn, help us when they intercede for us in return. Set aside time for them each day to pray or work for them.

Chapter 5
If You Want To Avoid Purgatory

Many Catholics do not consider the existence of Purgatory. This is mainly due to a poor understanding of this doctrine. It is thought that after death one goes either directly to Heaven or Hell. Those who do understand Purgatory believe that it is very difficult if not impossible to avoid it. Fortunately, Our Lord has provided the means to bypass Purgatory and go straight to Heaven.

The reason why Purgatory exists is that in order to go to Heaven, we must be perfectly free of sin since **"nothing unclean will enter it"**(Revelation 21:27). Every sin that is committed leaves a stain of sin that remains even after we repent and receive forgiveness from it.

The first and most important way to avoid Purgatory is to deal with its primary cause, that is, sin. It is sin that stains our souls and this stain must be removed before we can enter Heaven.

There are two types of sin: venial and mortal. They are mentioned in 1 John 5:17, **"all wrongdoing is sin, but there is sin that is not deadly"**. The sins that are not deadly are the venial ones. They are minor offenses against God that do not destroy our relationship with Him but can lead to related mortal sins if they continue without repentance.

Many people do not consider the consequences of minor (venial) sins. After all, a small lie or distasteful joke won't prevent you from entering Heaven, right? Even venial sins stain the soul. These stains will keep us in Purgatory until they are fully expiated because **"you will not get out until you have paid the last penny"** (Matthew 5:25).

There are also degrees of venial sins. A sin that occurs due to habit is worse than one that happens due to a moment of weakness.

The other sin, mortal, destroys the relationship with God and will lead to eternal separation from Him unless an act of contrition occurs. Three requirements must be met for a sin to be mortal:

1. the sin must be of a serious nature
2. the individual needs to be knowledgeable that the sin is serious
3. the individual must have the free will to commit the sin

If venial sins cause us to spend some time in Purgatory, mortal sins require a much greater purgatorial expiation. Why is this so severe? Considering that a single mortal sin can cause one to lose their salvation, this would be understandable why a great penance is needed.

When sins occurs, it needs to be forgiven. We can confess our sins directly to Jesus or we can confess our sins to Jesus through a priest. Why go to a priest to confess sin? After all, why not save yourself the embarrassment and confess to God privately? Jesus gave priests the authority to forgive sins, **"if you forgive anyone's sins, they are forgiven; if you retain anyone's sins, they are retained"** (John 20:23). In addition to having our sins forgiven by confessing to a priest, the priest can advise us how to avoid committing the same sin again in the future. You would not get this sort of guidance through private confession to God.

Once sin is forgiven, the stain of that sin remains on the soul. This stain needs to be removed in order to go to Heaven. We can purify our souls while on earth through penance, or we can do it painfully in Purgatory. When sin is confessed to a priest, a penance is given appropriate to the magnitude of the sin. This is another reason why frequent confession is beneficial.

The act of penance leads to an indulgence. This is what actually removes the punishment due to sin. An indulgence can either be **partial** (only part of the punishment is removed) or **plenary** (all of the punishment is removed). The majority of indulgences are partial since plenary ones are difficult to obtain. These are the steps to obtain a plenary indulgence:

1. the Sacrament of Reconciliation (or confession to a priest)
2. Holy Communion needs to be received
3. a prayer for the Pope's intention (this can be an *Our Father* and a *Hail Mary*).

No sin can be committed during this process or the indulgence will become partial.

A very good way to avoid Purgatory is to help those who are imprisoned there. The Holy Souls are aware of who prays for them and what role they played in lessening their time in Purgatory. Once they are released into Heaven, they pray constantly for the salvation of the those who helped them. Your time in Purgatory can be lessened if not eliminated by dedicating yourself to freeing the suffering saints. One great thing that can be done for them is to offer the indulgences from all of your prayers with the *Heroic Act of Charity*.

The final sacrament one receives, the *Sacrament of Extreme Unction*, can eliminate all of the time spent in Purgatory. The best thing that one can do with this sacrament is to offer it to the Holy Souls. Such a great deed would no doubt be repaid in a much greater way than if used for one's personal needs.

Part 2

Defending Purgatory

If one knew what we may obtain from God by the intercession of the Holy Souls, they would not be so much abandoned. Let us pray a great deal for them, they will pray for us.

St. John Vianney

Chapter 6
Answering Fundamentalists

There are 2.1 billions Christians in this world. We are the largest religious group and the closest rival are the 1.7 billion Muslims. Catholics number 1.3 billion and Protestants are around 350 million. In spite of the much larger number of Catholics, Protestants are very active in western nations. Many Catholics have been converted over to their faith, but this is mainly due to the Catholics ignorance of their own faith and being unable to respond to attacks against it. While this chapter will not be a complete course on Catholic apologetics, it will give you enough information to defend the doctrine of Purgatory.

Objection #1: Purgatory isn't mentioned in the Bible

Fundamentalists believe that the bible is the sole rule of faith (or *sola scriptura*). In other words, all Christian doctrine is in the bible. No other authoritative source is needed. So, the doctrine of Purgatory is to be rejected because they can't find it in the bible.

There is one small problem here. Sola scriptura is unbiblical. Fundamentalists believe that all of their doctrines are in the bible. The bible even says that not all doctrines are in the bible.

Fundamentalists believe in the doctrine of the trinity and the divinity of the holy spirit, but neither of these doctrines are in the bible. The first time the trinity was mentioned by a Christian was 190 AD by Tertullian. While the word, Purgatory, is not in the Bible, there are many passages that allude to its existence.

1 Corinthians 3:15 is the most commonly used biblical passage that Catholics use to show the existence of Purgatory: **"the one whose work is burnt down will suffer the loss of it, though he himself will be saved; he will be saved as someone might expect to be saved from a fire."**

Blaspheming the Holy Spirit will not be forgiven in this world, or the next: **"And anyone who says a word against the Son of man will be forgiven; but no one who speaks against the Holy Spirit will be forgiven either in this world or in the next"** (Matthew 12:32). This implies that there is another world where sins can be forgiven. It can't be Heaven where there is no sin, or Hell where there is no repentance, but it must be a third place where sins can be forgiven (i.e. Purgatory).

Another passage talks about a place where you will not be released until you paid your debt: **"In truth I tell you, you will not get out till you have paid the last penny"** (Matthew 5:26).

Jesus spoke about an unforgiving debtor would be tortured until he paid his debt. He said that the same thing would happen to us if we didn't forgive sins against us: **"And in his anger the master handed him over to the torturers till he should pay all his debt. And that is how my heavenly Father will deal with you unless you each forgive your brother from your heart"** (Matthew 18:34-35).

Nothing unclean can enter Heaven: **"Nothing unclean may come into it: no one who does what is loathsome or false, but only those who are listed in the Lamb's book of life"** (Revelation 21:27). If you die with unrepented sin, or are attached to worldly things, your not clean enough to enter Heaven. These things need to be purged from you before you can enter. The purging takes place in Purgatory.

Objection #2: There is no need for Purgatory. Jesus paid the price for our sins.

The Protestant view of salvation is very different from the Catholic one. They believe that Christ's death on the cross completely redeemed mankind and therefore there is no need for the expiation of sins in Purgatory. They believe that Catholics claim that the redemption of Christ was incomplete which is why we believe in Purgatory. There is, therefore, no need to pay for sins and suffer in Purgatory because Jesus already paid for them in full.

"Now I rejoice in my sufferings for your sake, and in my flesh I complete what is lacking in Christ's afflictions for the sake of his body, that is, the church" (Col 1:24). Ronald Knox interpreted this passage as *"the obvious meaning is that Christ's sufferings, although fully satisfactory on behalf of our sins, leave us under a debt of honor, as it were, to repay them by sufferings of our own"*. We must suffer for our sins, either here on earth or in Purgatory.

Objection #3: Purgatory wasn't believed by the early Christians. It was invented centuries later by the Catholic Church.

Fundamentalists believe that the early church was non-denominational. They weren't Baptists, Presbyterians, Pentecostals, and certainly not Catholics. The first followers of Christ were just Christians who used the bible as their sole rule of faith. The early church seems to be exactly like the Protestants who started 16 centuries later.

Catholicism is believed to have been started in 313 A.D. with the Edict of Milan by Constantine. After that, the real Christians went into hiding where they would reappear 1200 years later and claim that they were there all this time.

Since Purgatory is a Catholic doctrine, Fundamentalists claim that the early Christians didn't believe in this doctrine. However, there is evidence that the early church prayed for the dead. The catacombs in the first century had inscriptions requesting prayers for the dead. The first Christians were Jewish converts who had already had a long tradition of praying for the dead. There aren't any records of Christians protesting against these devotions. This is a time when any heresy led to a violent reaction from the then extremely conservative proto-Christians.

Objection #4: Praying for the dead is unbiblical.

The Jews have been praying for the dead before the time of Christ: **"For had he not expected the fallen to rise again, it would have been superfluous and foolish to pray for the dead, whereas if he had in view the splendid recompense reserved for those who make a pious end, the thought was holy and devout. Hence, he had this expiatory sacrifice offered for the dead, so that they might be released from their sin"** (2 Maccabees 12:44-45). This is a biblical text with Jews praying for the dead.

Even today, the Jews pray for the dead.

Objection #5: The Church uses Purgatory to make money.

If Purgatory is a money making scheme, it isn't a very good one. A mass for the dead typically costs $10 for a donation, but this amount isn't fixed and can be set to a lower amount or waved if the priest feels the parishioner can't afford it. Most of these Masses take place on days outside the Sunday services, where no collection is taken.

Considerably more money is generated on a Sunday Mass where you have hundreds of people donating money. Masses for the dead are definitely not a money maker.

Chapter 7
Historically Speaking

Most Protestants reject the doctrine of Purgatory, believing it to be both unbiblical and an invention of the Catholic Church. They think that the Christians of the early church did not believe in Purgatory or pray for the dead, and these doctrines were created by a corrupted paganized version of Christianity (the Catholic Church) centuries later.

What did the early Church believe and what did the Church Fathers teach? If Purgatory was invented by the Catholic Church, then there should be a time when this doctrine appeared. It does not necessarily have to be a fixed date. Protestants can have a good argument against Purgatory by showing a period when the doctrine was taught and a period before when there was no mention of it, implying it was created after that.

Purgatory did not always exist. To confirm Protestant beliefs, Purgatory is a Catholic invention. Now, to disappoint our separated brethren, the doctrine was not invented in the 6th Century by Pope St. Gregory III. Purgatory was created by God after Jesus died on the cross. Before Jesus' redemptive work on the cross, no one was able to enter Heaven. All those who died before the Crucifixion and were worthy of Heaven but could not enter due to the stain of sin waited in a place referred to as the *Limbo of the Fathers*.

Limbo is a state (or a place) between Heaven and Hell. The word came from *Limbus*, a Latin word meaning border. Before the Messiah came, no one could go to Heaven directly because nothing unclean may enter it (Revelation 21:27). Jesus had not yet died for their sins and redeemed them, so they were not worthy to be in God's presence. After Jesus died, **"He went to preach to the spirits in prison"** (1 Peter 3:19) and opened the way to Heaven for them. The prison was Limbo. After the gateway was opened to Heaven from Limbo, Purgatory was created. This was necessary because even though redemption is for all of mankind, many people leave this world unworthy to directly enter Heaven due to the stain of sin in their souls.

There were religious groups throughout history who have rejected Purgatory. In the early centuries after Christ, the Gnostics had no use for expiating their sins in an afterlife. They believed that the sufferings on earth were sufficient to purify their souls for Heaven.

The heretics of Arianism in the 4th Century believed that praying for the dead was immoral. Their reasoning behind this is that by doing so a person could commit any sin they wished and count on others praying for their soul in Purgatory.

The 12th Century had its share of doubters as well. The Waldenses had great disagreements among themselves over whether Purgatory was a reality. The influence of Gnosticism was still present in this era among the Albigenses and Catharers, both groups finding Purgatory to be incompatible with their doctrines.

The best known attack on the doctrine of Purgatory was by Martin Luther, a Catholic monk in the 16th Century. He began by attacking the pious practice of indulgences when he nailed his *"Disputation on the Power and Efficacy of Indulgences"* (more commonly known as *"The 95 Theses"*) on the door of the church beside the castle of Wittemburg in 1517. Luther did this on the day before All Saints Day. At that time there were abuses in indulgences which led Luther to publicly condemn them, but he went too far in his condemnation by attacking the authority of the Church to grant indulgences.

On that historic date, Luther had not condemned Purgatory. He believed in it but did not accept the Church's methods of obtaining indulgences for the poor souls there. From 1518-1519 he believed Purgatory was true and taught it to his followers. From there up to 1530 he kept the doctrine of Purgatory but did not want it to be an article of faith since he believed that it could neither be proved nor disproved but it should be permitted to be taught. In 1530, Luther published *"Denial of Purgatory"* which was his rejection of this ancient doctrine. He referred to Purgatory as a "Devil's mask" in the Schmalkaldian Articles of 1537. Luther did have varying opinions of Purgatory after that and in 1543 he allowed prayers for the dead in his "Church Directory".

There are of course more examples of Christians and non-Christians who reject Purgatory. Their main point is that they believe this doctrine was invented by the Catholic Church. Many point to Pope St. Gregory III instituting it in the 6th Century, but all of them would agree that it occurred after the 4th Century when the Catholic Church supposedly began. Since this doctrine began after the 4th Century, there should of course be no Christians praying for the dead before that and if there were, they would be condemned by the Church of that time.

There is no historical evidence of the Church condemning Purgatory or condemning prayers for dead before the 4th Century. There were prayers for the poor souls in Purgatory inscribed in the catacombs (underground tombs) in the first century.

In "The Acts of Paul and Thecla" (8:5-6; 160 A.D.), *"After the beasts had been shown, Trifina took Thecla home with her, and they went to bed. And behold, the daughter of Trifina, who was dead, appeared to her mother and said: Mother, let the young woman Thecla be reputed by you as your daughter in my place, and ask her to pray for me, that I may be translated to a state of happiness. Upon which Trifina, with a mournful air, said, My daughter Falconilla has appeared to me and ordered me to receive you in her place; wherefore I desire, Thecla, that you would pray for my daughter that she may be translated into a state of happiness and to life eternal"*. The idea here is prayers are requested to expiate Falconilla's sins so that she can go to Heaven sooner from Purgatory. Falconilla appeared to her mother and asked her bring Thecla into her household to pray for her soul.

Again, in the 2nd Century, more evidence of prayers for the dead, this time prayers being requested by a man planning for the future by requesting prayers for his soul while in Purgatory. *"The citizen of a prominent city, I erected this while I lived, that I might have a resting place for my body. Abercius is my name, a disciple of the chaste shepherd who feeds his sheep on the mountains and in the fields, who has great eyes surveying everywhere, who taught me the faithful writings of life. Standing by, I, Abercius, ordered this to be inscribed; truly I was in my seventy-second year. May everyone who is in accord with this and who understands it pray for Abercius"* (Epitaph of Abercius; 190 A.D.).

Tertullian wrote about Matthew 5:21-26. There Jesus taught about temporary and eternal punishment for sin. The temporary punishment would be in Purgatory, the other in Hell. The "prison" he talks about is Purgatory. This interpretation of this passage of Matthew was taught since the earliest times of the Church. *"To sum up, since that 'prison' which the Gospel indicates we understand to mean the place of the departed, and the 'last penny' we interpret to mean even a small fault which must be expiated there before the resurrection, no one shall doubt that the soul will pay something in the place of the departed spirits before the fullness of the resurrection in the flesh"* (On the Soul, 58; 208 A.D.).

He also wrote about making sacrifices for the dead on their birthdays. *"As often as the anniversary comes round, we make offerings for the dead as birthday honours"* (The Chaplet, 3; 211 A.D.).

Tertullian again writes, *"A woman, after the death of her husband ... prays for his soul and asks that he may, while waiting, find rest; and that he may share in the first resurrection. And each year, on the anniversary of his death, she offers the sacrifice"* (Monogamy 10:1-2; 216 A.D.).

And in 253 A.D., St. Cyprian wrote about Purgatory and also made a reference to Matthew 5:21-26, *"it is one thing, when cast into prison, not to go out thence until one has paid the uttermost farthing"*. "Farthing" is another way of saying a small amount of currency, such as a penny. The great saint has more to say on purification in Purgatory, *"it is one thing, tortured by long suffering for sins, to be cleansed and long purged by fire; another to have purged all sins by suffering. It is one thing, in fine, to be in suspense till the sentence of God at the day of judgment; another to be at once crowned by the Lord""*. These quotes can be found in St. Cyprian's Letters 51:20.

Those who claim that the Catholic Church started in the 4th Century say that it began in 313 with the Edict of Milan, so we can squeeze another quote by Lactantius from 307 A.D. *"But when He shall have judged the righteous, He will also try them with fire. Then they whose sins shall exceed either in weight or in number, shall be scorched by the fire and burnt: but they whom full justice and maturity of virtue has imbued will not perceive that fire; for they have something of God in themselves which repels and rejects the violence of the flame"*(Divine Institutes 7:21).

History shows us plenty of evidence that the early Church taught and believed in praying for the dead in Purgatory. What we won't find is the Church condemning these people as heretics for their teachings. These doctrines can be traced back to the origins of Christianity. However, talking about the history of Purgatory without doing something about the poor souls is useless. Remember to pray each day for them so that they can enter Heaven sooner. God will bless you for this and the souls you have freed will be eternally grateful.

Part 3

Odds and Ends

The holy souls are eager for the prayers of the faithful which can gain indulgences for them. Their intercession is powerful. Pray unceasingly. We must empty Purgatory!

Padre Pio

Chapter 8
The Heroic Act

The Merriam-Webster dictionary defines a hero as a *"mythological or legendary figure of great strength or ability; or a man admired for his achievements and qualities"*. A hero goes above and beyond the call of duty to help others. It is someone who has made a sacrifice for the benefit of those who could not help themselves.

There are heroes in the Catholic Church. These are the canonized saints. It is true that all people who enter Heaven are saints, but the canonized ones have done something that is extraordinary and have been made role models for future generations of Christians.

All of us can become heroes while on earth. It won't necessarily lead to our canonization, but it would definitely help those in need and also bring us closer to Jesus. An opportunity has been given to us by the Church to help the souls in Purgatory: it is the Heroic Act of Charity.

Through the Heroic Act, we provide all of the indulgences from our prayers, our sufferings, and our works of charity for the benefit of the souls in Purgatory. Also, the indulgences from the prayers offered after your death will go to the souls in Purgatory. Even though we give the holy souls the value of our indulgenced acts, we still keep the blessings of what we have done which will bring us glory in Heaven.

The Heroic Act of Charity was approved by Popes Benedict XIII (1728), Pius VI (1788), and Pius XI (1852). The Sacred Congregation of Indulgences made a decree regarding it on December 18, 1885, and it was confirmed by Pope Leo XIII the next day:

> "The Heroic Act of Charity in favor of the souls detained in purgatory consists in this, that a member of the Church militant (Christifidelis), either using a set formula or simply by an act of his will, offers to God for the souls in purgatory all the satisfactory works which he will perform during his lifetime, and also all the suffrages which may accrue to him after his death. Many Christians devoted to the Blessed Virgin Mary, acting on the advice of the Theatine Regular Cleric Father Gaspar Olider, of blessed memory, make it a practice to deposit the said merits and suffrages as it were into the hands of the Blessed Virgin that she may distribute these favors to the souls in Purgatory according to her own merciful pleasure."
>
> Decree of the Sacred Congregation of Indulgences

You might be thinking, "What a great idea, but what will happen to me when I die, and I don't have any indulgences to get me out of Purgatory? Will I suffer enormously there because of the Heroic Act?" This objection is not taking into account God's love and mercy for us:

> "If anyone wants to be a follower of mine, let him renounce himself and take up his cross and follow me. Anyone who wants to save his life will lose it; but anyone who loses his life for my sake will find it."
>
> Matthew 16: 24-25

We would be blessed by God for making this sacrifice. St. Gertrude the Great (who revealed the prayer to release 1000 souls from Purgatory) made this heroic act. When she was close to death, the sins she had committed came to her mind along with the fact that she gave all of her indulgences to the souls in Purgatory. The devil tormented her by showing that she would suffer a great deal in Purgatory because she didn't have anything to help her get out sooner. At that point, Jesus appeared to her and said, *"Be assured, My daughter, your charity towards the departed will be no detriment to you. Know that the generous donation you have made of all your works to the holy souls has been singularly pleasing to Me; and to give you a proof thereof, I declare to you that all the pains you would have had to endure in the other life are now remitted; moreover, in recompense for your generous charity, I will so enhance the value of the merits of your works as to give you a great increase of glory in Heaven."*

In the past, there were a series of indulgences that benefited those who made the Heroic Act of Charity, but these indulgences have not been mentioned in the Enchiridion of Indulgences (Sacred Apostolic Penitentiary; June 29, 1968) so they may not be in effect at this time. This should not in any way prevent us from performing this Act. The goal here is to help the souls in Purgatory any way we can.

If you would like to make the Heroic Act, you can in your own words offer the indulgences of all your prayers, your works of charity, and your sufferings for the benefit of the souls in Purgatory. This includes the benefits of all of the prayers said for you after death. If you have a problem with saying this in your own words, use the following prayer:

> *Lord Jesus, King of Infinite Mercy, I give all of the indulgences that would have been mine through my prayers, acts of charity, my own sufferings, and for the prayers said for me when I pass into eternity to free my brothers and sisters from the pains of Purgatory. Have mercy on them and bring them into glory in Your eternal presence in Heaven.*
>
> *Amen.*

Praying for the dead is a spiritual work of mercy. With the Heroic Act of Charity, we can help the poor souls in a much more effective way. I highly recommend that all Catholics who love the souls in Purgatory do this act of mercy.

Chapter 9
The Enchiridion of Indulgences

The first question you are probably wondering is what is an "enchiridion"? For a quick definition, it means a collection. The next question is why would theologians give a name like that to a book. The answer is that people who are very well educated like to confuse people outside their field with terms that make sense only to them. Humor aside, the *Enchiridion of Indulgences* is actually a marvelous book containing the Church's revised collection of indulgenced prayers and acts. The sad thing about this book is that few Catholics have seen it or heard of it and even fewer know how to spell it.

Contrary to popular opinion, Vatican II did not do away with indulgences. This doctrine was reviewed and it was later disregarded as irrelevant by many Catholics. The Enchiridion was released in 1968 under the difficult to pronounce Latin name of "Enchiridion Indulgentiarum" by the Sacred Apostolic Penitentiary. Pope Paul VI gave his full approval of the book on June 15th of that year and it then went into mass production (no pun intended) by the Vatican Press.

Indulgences were revised in that only the "most important works of prayer and works of piety, charity, and penance" (Enchiridion, Preliminary Observations, 1) had an indulgence. A greater emphasis was made on works of piety, while the overall number of indulgences have been reduced. It was hoped that this would inspire Catholics to do more works of charity and become closer to God. The Enchiridion states that *"the main concern has been to attach greater importance to a Christian way of life and to lead souls to cultivate the spirit of prayer and penance and to practice the theological virtues, rather than merely to repeat certain formulas and acts."* It makes sense. St. Thomas of Aquinas preferred to give alms (a free gift given to help relieve the poor) before fasting and penance. He said that *"alms giving possesses more completely the virtue of satisfaction than prayer.* St. James also placed a great deal of emphasis on action by saying how a person can be **"justified by works and not by faith alone"** (James 2:24). Prayer is a wonderful thing, but we also need to get our hands dirty and perform acts of charity for God as well.

If you would like to learn which prayers and works have indulgences, get a copy of the Enchiridion of Indulgences. It is also available for free on Internet at various web sites, do a search for it and you'll find it. A book like this can only bring you closer to God.

Chapter 10
Indulgences on the High Seas

You want to gain a Jubilee indulgence. That's great. There's one problem. You noticed that your surrounded by water and there doesn't seem to be any floating cathedrals or churches anywhere nearby. This is the dilemma of people who work on ships and even those who are on cruise vacations.

But its the Catholic Church to the rescue. In the *Paenitentiaria Apostolica* (given in Rome on November 1, 1999), it provided a way to receive the indulgence while on a ship. All that you have to do is pray the *Our Father* and *Apostles Creed* before a religious image. You also need to renounce all sin and have the intention to receive communion and go to confession as soon as possible. Of course, prayers for the Pope's intentions should be made and that is normally an *Our Father* and a *Hail Mary*.

Chapter 11
Jubilee Indulgences

The last Jubilee was declared by the Church in the year 2000. In this year, a new set of indulgences has been declared for this Jubilee and future ones (the next one likely to be in 2050). With the new indulgences, we can do a great deal to help release the holy souls from Purgatory.

It is not known where the word Jubilee came from but it may have originated from the Hebrew word *yobel*, which translates to "rams horn". This horn was used by the Jews for proclaiming a celebration or a time of rejoicing.

The year of the Jubilee began in the Old Testament times. In Leviticus 25:10, we read **"you will declare this fiftieth year to be sacred and proclaim the liberation of all the country's inhabitants"**. Every fifty years, God had commanded the Israelites to return to their own ancestral lands and leave any properties they owned outside of it. They had to sell the land (at a reasonable price) to their ancestral owners. The Jews were also required not to harvest their lands during that year. They were to eat whatever their fields would produce. Slaves were also to be released at this time and debts were to be forgiven. In short, the Jubilee was a time of remission or universal pardon. Truly, this was a time for rejoicing. God had promised great blessings (Leviticus 25:18-19) for those who fulfilled their Jubilee obligations.

The Jubilee today is a spiritualized form of the Old Testament version. The first Christian Jubilee was started in 1300 by Pope Boniface VIII. While the original Jubilee dealt with material things, the new Jubilee was about the remission of personal sin, and of course, indulgences which can be used to help the souls in Purgatory. The type of indulgence received is a plenary indulgence and this can completely free the recipient of the punishments due to their sins. They can apply it to themselves or to someone in Purgatory. The *Decree of the Sacred Penitentiary On the Conditions for Gaining the Jubilee Indulgence*(presented in Rome at the Apostolic Penitentiary on November 29, 1998) stated that applying a Jubilee indulgence to someone in Purgatory is *"an outstanding act of supernatural charity, in virtue of the bond which, in the Mystical Body of Christ, unites the faithful still on pilgrimage here below and those who have already ended their earthly journey"*. A plenary indulgence given to a soul in Purgatory would instantly free them and allow them to enter Heaven.

In order to get the indulgence, the following requirements must be fulfilled: sacramental confession, receive communion, perform the indulgenced act (i.e. pilgrimage, charity, penitence, etc.), and prayers for the Pope's intentions (usually an Our Father and a Hail Mary). Also, you need to be in a state of grace, you must be a baptized Catholic and not excommunicated from the Church, the intention must be there to try to gain the indulgence, and here's the difficult part, you need to be free from all sin including venial sin. A holy state is necessary to get a plenary indulgence. Even though this may be difficult to do, you should try anyways. If you don't get the plenary indulgence, a partial one will be gained which can also help the holy souls.

You can get one plenary indulgence per day and you can receive an unlimited number of partial indulgences each day. You don't have to receive communion or go to confession each day to get the Jubilee indulgence. Communion can be received several days before or after the indulgenced act, and confession can also be made within several days of the indulgence. What does several days mean, well, with confession it is generally thought of as eight days.

The main way to receive the Jubilee indulgence is through a pilgrimage to a religious shrine. For those who are in Rome, they can make their pilgrimage to one of the four Patriarchal Basilicas (the Basilica of Saint Peter in the Vatican, the Basilica of Saint Mary Major, the Archbasilica of the Most Holy Saviour at the Lateran, and the Basilica of Saint Paul on the Ostian Way). Once there, they can take part in a Mass or some other pious devotion (Stations of the Cross, Rosary, etc.). The other shrines in Rome are the Basilica of the Holy Cross in Jerusalem, the Shrine of Our Lady of Divine Love, the Basilica of Saint Lawrence in Campo Verano, and the Christian Catacombs in Rome.

If you are in Israel, you can make your pilgrimage to the Basilica of the Holy Sepulchre in Jerusalem, the Basilica of the Annunciation in Nazareth, or the Basilica of the Nativity in Bethlehem.

A pilgrimage can also be made to your local Cathedral or other churches designated by your bishop. Another thing that you can do is visit the needy (people who are sick, elderly, disabled, imprisoned, etc.) and do this as if making a pilgrimage to Christ within them.

Those who are in religious orders and cannot travel in a pilgrimage can visit the chapel in their residence or if this is not possible, they may unite themselves with those making a pilgrimage and offer their prayers and sufferings to God.

A pilgrimage is not necessary to gain the indulgence. It can also be attained by fasting (giving up food, social media, etc.), donating money to the poor, helping a religious or social cause, or any other type of personal sacrifice.

The requirements for the Jubilee indulgence here have been summarized and you should contact your local parish for more information on how to receive the indulgence. In any case, we have been given another opportunity to help the holy souls and we should take full advantage when the Church declares a year to be a Jubilee.

Chapter 12
Catholics and Halloween?

October 31. Halloween. An event that children anticipate all year, but parents view as another set of expenses buying costumes and candy for trick or treaters. Children enjoy this day because they are allowed to dress ridiculously and collect large amounts of candy which should last one or two months if they carefully budget their junk food eating.

For those not familiar with the modern Western tradition of Halloween, it is a peculiar custom where children dress up in some type of costume, a hero they have, a monster, or whatever their overactive imaginations can think of, and then they go door to door asking for candy. Actually, what they usually say is, *"Trick or Treat"*. What they want is the treat, meaning the candy or anything else that is unhealthy and tastes good. In most cases, they get the treat. In some instances, the people in the home pretend they're not there and don't answer the door. For those foolish enough not to answer the door and give a treat, they must face the wrath of the costumed children, in other words, this is the trick. This can entail acts along the lines of eggs (usually raw or soft boiled) thrown at various parts of the house, or other terrible things which we won't discuss here so that we don't give any ideas to any kids who read this article. Note that the trick part usually isn't played, not only because of the legal ramifications of vandalism, but mainly because the kids have a lot of ground to cover and don't want to waste time with those not willing to play ball.

This sounds harmless enough. Just a fun time for children to collect candy and generated more business for dentists down the road. It shouldn't bother anyone, right? Wrong. Conservative

Christians, mainly Fundamentalists, see Halloween and in particular, All Saints Day, as pagan in origin and therefore evil. No one who calls themselves a Christian should participate in this festival. Where did our Christian brethren get this idea from? Is Halloween really an evil tradition that should be avoided?

The concept of Halloween came from an old fire festival courtesy of the Celtics. The Celts were a pagan people who lived on the British Isles, Ireland, and northwest France. The festival was called *Samhain*, pronounced "sow-in", where "sow" is pronounced like "cow". The Celts celebrated this festival at the end of each summer. According to their spiritual beliefs, they believed this day to be the most effective time to communicate with their deceased family and friends.

The word Halloween was derived from the British day called *All Hallows* on November 1st, where the previous day was called *All Hallows Eve*. The day of November 1 was also known as *Hallowmas*. The purpose of All Saints Day is not to pray for the souls in Purgatory, as many misinformed people believe. It is meant for honoring ALL saints, both known and unknown. Most saints are ignored or don't receive the proper veneration due to them. This day brings the Church together to honor them.

The next day, All Souls Day, is meant to pray for and honor those holy souls who are in Purgatory. All Souls Day would normally occur on November 2 unless this day is a Sunday or a solemnity, where in that case it would be moved to the next day. On that day, there is usually a special Mass to pray for our beloved family and friends in Purgatory.

The veneration of saints was practiced from the earliest periods of Church history. The early Christians honored the greatest of the martyred saints on the anniversary of their deaths at the location they were martyred. By the fourth century, neighboring dioceses began sharing their relics with each other for the veneration of their saints and they also made common days when they would be honored. When Diocletian (284-305 A.D.) persecuted Christians, there were so many martyrs that each could not have a separate day assigned to them, so a common day was applied to all. Evidence of this common day was found in Antioch (the first Sunday after Pentecost), the sermon of St. Ephrem the Syrian (373 A.D.), and from St. John Chrysostom's 74th homily (407 A.D.).

The first steps towards a universal day to honor the saints occurred when the Pantheon of Rome was consecrated to the Blessed Virgin and all of the martyrs by Pope St. Boniface IV in May 13, 609 or 610 (it is not known which of these years it took place in). The pope also set aside an anniversary to honor these saints. Pope St. Gregory III (731-741 A.D.) started the feast of All Saints on November 1st with the consecration of a chapel in the basilica of St. Peter for all the saints.

Christians have been praying for the Holy Souls in Purgatory from the time of the Apostles. Benedictine monasteries had a common day of pray for their members in Purgatory annually in the 6th Century. In 7th Century Spain, the first Saturday before Pentecost was when they honored the poor souls. Germans also had an annual devotion for the souls which occurred on October 1st in the 10th Century. This devotion spread throughout the Church and eventually it was set on November 2nd as All Souls Day.

So what's the big fuss about? Why do conservative Christians oppose Halloween and All Saints/Souls Day? Since Halloween itself is pagan in origin, coming from Samhain, they reject it simply because they believe that anything pagan is evil (although many of them have no objection to the pagan custom of wedding rings). They also oppose the Catholic feast days of Nov. 1 and 2 because they involve honoring and praying to Saints, and praying for the souls in Purgatory. Devotion to saints and the existence of Purgatory are denied by our Protestant brothers since they claim that these are Catholic "inventions". What they don't realize is that these doctrines have been taught by Christians before

Protestant Reformers rejected them in the 16th Century. One has to only read the writings of the early Church Fathers to see this.

The unfortunate thing about Halloween is that an opportunity exists for those opposed to Catholicism to attack it. By pointing out the pagan origins of Halloween and pointing to All Saints Day, they try to plant the seeds of doubt in Catholic minds in an attempt to convert them to their own belief system. It should be remembered that history supports the Catholic side. The practices of Christians throughout the ages confirms that they prayed to saints and also for the souls in Purgatory. There is also biblical evidence which points towards prayers benefiting the dead. Jesus also promised that the Church would be free from doctrinal error. He told Peter that the **"gates of the netherworld shall not prevail against it"** (Matthew 16:18). Praying to saints and belief in Purgatory are most certainly valid Christian beliefs.

Don't be concerned over All Saints Day and All Souls Day. These are wonderful times to remember the saints and the poor souls. Remember to pray for the souls in Purgatory, since it is a **"holy and pious thought"** (2 Maccabees 12:45) to do so. Also, don't just pray for the souls once a year, there are many of our brothers and sisters in Purgatory and we should pray for them each day. Encourage your family and friends to do so as well. Remember, one day you may be in Purgatory and you would then want people to pray for you.

Chapter 13
Gregorian Masses

An ancient but mostly unknown custom of the Church is the offering of a daily Mass for 30 days for a soul in Purgatory. After the Masses are said, the soul would immediately be freed from Purgatory and enter Heaven.

As its name implies, Gregorian Masses were named after St. Gregory the Great who was the pope from 590 to 604 A.D. This traditional sequence of Masses was not started by St. Gregory but became popular when he promoted it.

In his Dialogues, St. Gregory wrote that he had one Mass said each day over 30 days for the soul of Justus (a monk who had recently died). After the last Mass was said for him, he appeared to his brother, Copiosus, to tell him the good news of his departure from Purgatory into Heaven. Copiosus did not know about the 30 Masses that were said for his brother. He found out about them later when he spoke to the monks about his brother's deliverance.

In the church of Sts. Andrew and Gregory (located on Mt. Coelius, where Justus had died in the convent of St. Andrew), there is an inscription of a private revelation that St. Gregory received on the benefits of 30 consecutive Masses for a soul in Purgatory.

It is not known why Gregorian Masses would release a soul from Purgatory. The custom of praying 30 days for the dead can be traced back to the Old Testament. The Jews prayed for 30 days after the death of Moses according to their **"days of weeping for the mourning rites"** (Deuteronomy 34:8).

Gregorian Masses spread throughout Europe and many Religious Orders. It unfortunately faded after the Protestant Reformation and the French Revolution, but the love Catholics have for the holy souls gradually brought back this practice.

The way the Masses are to be said is once per day for 30 consecutive days. They can only be said for one person at a time who is in Purgatory. If the blessed soul is already in Heaven, the indulgences may be applied to another needy soul according to God's infinite mercy.

The Masses must be said one day after another without any interruption. The exception to this is if the last three days of Holy Week occur during the Gregorian Masses. If this is the case, then the Masses may be stopped until Easter Sunday and then continued on that day. The 30 Masses cannot all be Masses of Requiem. They can also be said at any altar.

Now here comes the difficult part. The problem with Gregorian Masses is that because 30 Masses are required, it becomes expensive to pay for all of them. A stipend is offered to the priest who presides over the Mass and the cost is normally $10 (Canada, USA). This would make the total cost for the Gregorian Masses at $300. This is not to say that you can buy someone out of Purgatory. The stipend is a free will offering for the priest to do the Mass. Of course, depending on the financial circumstances of the people requesting the Masses, a priest may lower or not require any payment at all for the them.

Another problem is that most parish priests will not have the time to do a daily Mass for an individual in Purgatory. A solution to this is to find a priest who is retired or contact a monastery where you can usually find priests and monks available for Gregorian Masses.

In any case, if Gregorian Masses can be done then it is a great blessing for a soul in Purgatory. If the cost is too high, there are other effective ways to free souls from Purgatory, such as praying for them in Masses, rosaries, novenas, charitable works, etc. Gregorian Masses are but one option we Catholics have to help those in Purgatory.

Chapter 14
Divine Mercy for the Holy Souls

> "... After eight days [after the Feast of Easter] let there be another feast observed with honor, the eighth day itself on which He [Jesus] gave me Thomas, who was hard of belief, full assurance, by showing me the print of the nails, and the wound made in His side by the spear."
>
> St. Thomas the Apostle, writing in The Apostolic Constitutions (Book 5, Chapter 19)

In 1931, Sister Faustina (now a canonized saint) received a vision of Our Lord. Jesus was clothed in a white robe and His right hand was making a blessing while the left was touching His heart. From that point, two large rays of light were emitted. One was red and the other was pale. St. Faustina stared at Jesus with awe and with great joy. Our Lord then said asked her to paint the image of Him that she saw with the text **"Jesus, I trust in You"** at the bottom. A promise was made that those who venerate this image would not perish and they would also have victory over their enemies, especially at the hour of death. What followed over the next several years were extensive apparitions from Jesus on Divine Mercy.

One request from Our Lord was to establish a feast the first Sunday after Easter, *"Yes the first Sunday after Easter is the Feast of Mercy, but there must also be acts of mercy, and I demand the worship of My mercy through the solemn celebration of the Feast and through the veneration of the image which is painted. By means of this image I shall grant many graces to souls. It is to be a reminder of the demands of My mercy, because even the strongest faith is of no avail without works"* (742).

On this day, a remarkable event would take place. Our Lord said that *"the soul that will go to Confession and receive Holy Communion shall obtain complete forgiveness of sins and punishment. I want to grant a complete pardon to the souls that will go to Confession and receive Holy Communion on the Feast of My Mercy"* (Diary 1109). In other words, a plenary indulgence may be obtained on the Feast of Divine Mercy.

Just imagine. All of your sins that would have led to a lengthy time of expiation in Purgatory can be forgiven. You can skip Purgatory and go straight to Heaven, assuming that you don't sin from that point onwards. All of your sins up to that point will be forgiven.

For those interested in self improvement, this is a great thing to do. An even better thing to do with this indulgence is to transfer it to someone else, more specifically, someone in Purgatory. A partial indulgence given to a holy soul in Purgatory remits part of their sin, shortening their time there by a particular amount (depending on the nature of the indulgence). A plenary indulgence for a holy soul completely remits all of their sins and they immediately enter Heaven.

So, instead of applying the plenary indulgence from the Feast of Divine Mercy to yourself, give it to a suffering saint.

In order to make a plenary indulgence, three conditions must be met: go to confession, receive communion, and pray for the intentions of the Pope (usually an Our Father and Hail Mary). There is one catch, though. There can be no sin committed, not even a venial one, while attempting to make this indulgence. Doing so would turn the indulgence into a partial one. It's difficult to make a plenary indulgence. This is why it's a good idea to perform the conditions close to each other.

It may have been a long time since your last confession but this shouldn't prevent you from receiving the Sacrament of Reconciliation. Our Lord Jesus said, *"The soul that will go to Confession and receive Holy Communion shall obtain complete forgiveness of sins and punishment. On that day all the divine floodgates through which graces flow are opened. Let no soul fear to draw near to Me, even though its sins be as scarlet.... Mankind will not have peace until it turns to the Fount of My Mercy"* (699).

Helping a soul in Purgatory has other benefits. When we pray for them and lessen their time there, they in gratitude will pray for us. Padre Pio said that *"if one knew what we may obtain from God by the intercession of the Holy Souls, they would not be so much abandoned."* If our prayers will free a holy soul, they will pray unceasingly in Heaven for our salvation. So on the first Sunday after Easter, Divine Mercy Sunday, offer your plenary indulgence for a suffering saint and your future eternal life will be secured.

Chapter 15
I Urge Catholics to Pray for the Dead - Pope John Paul II

To the Most Reverend Raymond Séguy, Bishop of Autun, Châlon and Mâcon, Abbot of Cluny

1. This year, when we are celebrating the millennium of the Commemoration of All the Faithful Departed, established by St. Odilo, fifth Abbot of Cluny, the centenary of the foundation of the Archfraternity of Our Lady of Cluny, committed to praying for the souls in purgatory, and the 40th anniversary of the bulletin Lumière et vie, which promotes prayer for the dead, I gladly join in spirit all those who will take part this year in the celebrations offered for those who have gone before us. Indeed, on the day after the feast of All Saints, when the Church joyfully celebrates the communion of saints and human salvation, St. Odilo urged his monks to say special prayers for all the dead, thus mysteriously contributing to their entry into beatitude; the custom of solemnly interceding for the dead in a celebration which St. Odilo called All Souls Day gradually spread from the Abbey of Cluny and is now the practice throughout the universal Church.

2. In praying for the dead, the Church above all contemplates the mystery of the Resurrection of Christ, who obtains salvation and eternal life for us through his Cross. Thus with St. Odilo we can ceaselessly repeat: "The Cross is my refuge, my way and my life.... The Cross repels all evil. The Cross dispels the darkness". The Lord's Cross reminds us that all life is illumined by the light of Easter and that no situation is totally lost, for Christ conquered death and opened the way for us to true life. Redemption "is brought about in the sacrifice of Christ, by which man redeems

the debt of sin and is reconciled to God" (Tertio millennio adventitente, n. 7).

3. Our hope is founded on Christ's sacrifice. His Resurrection inaugurates the "end of the times" (1 Pet 1:20; cf. Heb 1:2). The belief in eternal life which we profess in the Creed is an invitation to the joyful hope of seeing God face to face. To believe in the resurrection of the flesh is to recognize that there is a final end, an ultimate goal for all human life, "which so satisfies man's appetite that nothing else is left for him to desire" (Thomas Aquinas, Summa Theologiae, I-II, q. 1, a. 5; St. Paulinus of Nola, Letters, 1, 2). This same desire is wonderfully expressed by St. Augustine: "You have made us for yourself, and our heart is restless until it rests in you" (Confessions, I, 1). Thus, we are all called to live with Christ, seated at the right hand of the Father, and to contemplate the Holy Trinity, for "God is the principal object of Christian hope" (Alphonsus Liguori, Practice of the Love of Jesus Christ, 16, 2); we can say with Job: "I know that my Redeemer lives, and at last he will stand upon the earth; and after my skin has been thus destroyed, then from my flesh I shall see God, whom I shall see on my side, and my eyes shall behold and not another" (Job 19:25-27).

4. Let us also remember that the Mystical Body of Christ is waiting to be reunited at the end of history, when all its members will be in perfect beatitude and God will be all in all (cf. Origen, Homilies on Leviticus, n. 7). In fact, the Church hopes for the eternal salvation of all her children and of all mankind. "We believe that the Church is necessary to salvation, for Christ is the one mediator and way of salvation and he becomes present to us in his Body which is the Church, but the divine design of salvation embraces all men. Those indeed who are in ignorance of Christ's Gospel and of his Church through no fault of their own, who search for God in sincerity of heart, and who, acting according to conscience, strive under the influence of grace to fulfill his will, belong to his people, even though in a way we cannot see, and can obtain eternal salvation. Their number is

known only to God" (Paul VI, Credo of the People of God, 30 June 1968).

While waiting for death to be overcome once and for all, "some of the disciples are pilgrims on earth. Others have died and are being purified, while still others are in glory", contemplating the Trinity in full light (Second Vatican Council, Lumen gentium, n. 49; cf. Eugene IV, Bull Laetantur coeli). Joined to the merits of the saints, our fraternal prayer comes to the aid of those who await the beatific vision. Intercession for the dead, just as the life of those living according to the divine commandments, obtains the merits that serve the full attainment of salvation. It is an expression of the fraternal charity of the one family of God, by which "we are faithful to the Church's deepest vocation" (Lumen gentium, n. 51): "to save souls who will love God eternally" (Thérèse of Lisieux, Prayers, 6; cf. Manuscript A 77). For the souls in purgatory, waiting for eternal happiness and for meeting the Beloved is a source of suffering, because of the punishment due to sin which separates them from God. But there is also the certitude that once the time of purification is over, the soul will go to meet the One it desires (cf. Ps 42:62).

5. Contemplation of the lives of those who have followed Christ encourages us to lead a good, upright Christian life which makes us "worthy of the kingdom of God" (2 Thes 1:5). Thus we are called to "supernatural vigilance", in the words of Cardinal Perraud (Lettra a l'occasion du neuvième centenaire de la fête pour les morts), so that we can prepare ourselves each day for eternal life. As Cardinal John Henry Newman emphasized: "We are not simply to believe, but to watch; not simply to love, but to watch; not simply to obey, but to watch; ... and thus it happens that watching is a suitable test of a Christian". This is because to watch is "to be detached from what is present, and to live in what is unseen; to live in the thought of Christ as he came once, and as he will come again; to desire his second coming" (Parochial and Plain Sermons, IV, 22).

6. The prayers of intercession and petition which the Church never ceases to raise to God have great value. They are "characteristic of a heart attuned to God's mercy" (Catechism of the Catholic Church, n. 2635). The Lord always lets himself be moved by his children's supplications, for he is the God of the living. During the Eucharist, through the general intercessions and the Memento for the dead, the assembled community presents to the Father of all mercies those who have died, so that through the trial of purgatory they will be purified, if necessary, and attain eternal joy. In entrusting them to the Lord, we recognize our solidarity with them and share in their salvation in this wondrous mystery of the communion of saints. The Church believes that the souls detained in purgatory "are helped by the prayers of the faithful and most of all by the acceptable sacrifice of the altar" (Council of Trent, Decree on Purgatory), as well as by "alms and other works of piety" (Eugene IV, Bull Laetantur coeli). "In fact, that same holiness, which is derived simply from their participation in the Church's holiness, represents their first and fundamental contribution to the holiness of the Church herself, which is the 'communion of saints'" (Christifideles laici, n. 17).

7. I therefore encourage Catholics to pray fervently for the dead, for their family members and for all our brothers and sisters who have died, that they may obtain the remission of the punishments due to their sins and may hear the Lord's call: "Come, O my dear soul, to eternal repose in the arms of my goodness, which has prepared eternal delights for you" (Francis de Sales, Introduction to the Devout Life, 17, 4).

As I entrust the faithful who will pray for the dead to the intercession of Our Lady, of St. Odilo and of St. Joseph, patron of a happy death, I cordially grant my Apostolic Blessing to them and to the members of the diocesan community of Autun, to the members of the Archconfraternity of Our Lady of Cluny and to the readers if Lumière et vie. I willingly extend it during the millennial year to all who pray for the intention of the souls in purgatory, who take part in the Eucharist and who offer sacrifices for the dead.

Chapter 16
Praying for the Holy Souls During Lent

The word "lent" is derived from the Old English term, "lencten" which means springtime. It's a period of 40 days (including 6 Sundays) which lasts from Ash Wednesday to the Vespers of Holy Saturday.

Lent is typically seen as a time for Catholics to give up something they enjoy for 40 days. You can read many articles on the Internet about how people are suffering because they're giving up chocolate or something along those lines. The attitude is, "oh no, another 40 days of pain because I have to make a sacrifice". I also found many blogs where Protestants attack the idea of us giving up food and of course they misquote the Bible to prove their point. They don't understand Lent either.

The purpose of this liturgical season is penance. Jesus fasted for 40 days, so we fast for the same period while waiting to celebrate His resurrection on Easter. Unfortunately, many Catholics focus on themselves during Lent. While reflecting on our spiritual life is important, this should also be a time to remember the holy souls in Purgatory.

There are many ways to help the suffering souls during Lent. Some of the things that you can do are:

- offer a mass for them
- pray the rosary or the way of the cross to release them Purgatory

- acts of charity on their behalf
- offer all of your indulgences to them through the Heroic Act

Being human, you may fail to fulfill your Lenten goals. If you do, remember that God is merciful. When you fail, don't beat yourself up, pick yourself up and continue the battle.

Chapter 17
Vain Repetition The Rosary and the Holy Souls

> **In your prayers do not babble as the gentiles do, for they think that by using many words they will make themselves heard.**
>
> Matthew 6:7

This is a favorite passage from the Bible that is used by Fundamentalists to condemn Catholics. They believe that reciting pre-written prayers and following liturgies are vain repetitions which Jesus condemns. The rosary is a prime target since it has many repeated prayers and the monotones which seem to confirm their belief that it is a mindless, meaningless prayer.

Is repeating a prayer over and over again vain repetition? In Heaven, there are four angelic beings praising God day and night, **"holy, holy, holy is the Lord God almighty, who was, and who is, and who is to come"** (Revelation 4:8). Repetitive prayer can also be found in Psalms 118 and 136. Repetitive prayer is not vain when you pray with your heart. Jesus condemned prayer that is made when the intent is to use many words to force a response from God.

The repetitive rosary we all know and love is not in the Bible. That is, the order of prayers with the prayer beads are not there. However, the prayers and meditations of the rosary are either taken directly from Scripture or are based on it.

The word rosary means a crown of roses, which is presented to Our Lady in prayer. A more precise term for it is the Dominican Rosary to separate it from the many forms of rosaries and chaplets out there (i.e. Chaplet of the Holy Wounds, Chaplet of Divine Mercy). The rosary in English has also been referred to as Our Lady s Psalter.

The common story where the rosary came from is that Our Lady appeared to St. Dominic in 1221 and gave it to him. Many historians take considerable delight in pointing out that there is no historical basis for this belief. The origins of the modern rosary would take place about two centuries later through a disciple of St. Dominic, Blessed Alain de la Roche. St. Dominic used an earlier form of the rosary to combat Albigensian heretics who were wreaking spiritual havoc in Europe.

The origins of the rosary can be traced back to the Psalms. Way back in those good old days, monks prayed the 150 Psalms as part of their daily devotions. The laity would have loved to pray this as well, but unfortunately, most of them were illiterate and the printing press wasn't around to mass-produce Bibles (which were at that time duplicated very expensively by hand). So to compromise, the laity prayed 150 Hail Marys for the Psalms. Gradually, these devotions evolved to the rosary of our time.

The rosary is a very powerful prayer. In fact, St. Alphonsus Liguori stressed the best way to help the souls in Purgatory, after having Masses said for them, is to pray rosaries and join the Confraternity of the Rosary. He also that if we want to help the souls in Purgatory and bring them great relief, we should recite the Rosary.

Mary plays a key role in the release of souls from Purgatory. St. Bernard referred to her as the Plenipotentiary, meaning one who is all powerful over Purgatory because she has the graces and power from God to free the souls there. We are all her children and like any good mother she takes care of us, especially those children who are suffering. Her intercession brings relief to the holy souls, as she related to Bl. Alain de la Roche: *"I am the Mother of the souls in Purgatory and every prayer on my account relieves the pains of my devotees".*

St. Pompilio Pirroti had a great devotion for the poor souls. When he prayed the rosary, the holy souls prayed along with him, shouting in response to each Hail Mary recited. The souls in Purgatory were tranquil and full of joy while the rosary was prayed.

St. Louis de Montfort in his book, *The Secret of the Rosary*, wrote about a woman delivered from Purgatory. A young lady of noble rank named Alexandra was converted by St. Dominic and enrolled in the Confraternity of the Rosary. When Alexandra died, she appeared to St. Dominic and told that him that she would have to spend the next 700 years in Purgatory to purify her soul because of the many sins in her life and also for leading others to commit sins by her poor example. She begged him and the Confraternity members to pray for her. He of course did so along with many other rosary devotees. Two weeks later, St. Dominic received another apparition of Alexandra. This time she was in full heavenly glory. She related that the intercessions through the rosary released her from Purgatory. She also told him that the holy souls begged him to continue preaching the rosary and to ask their relatives to pray for them using the rosary. The poor souls would greatly reward those who helped them when they entered Heaven.

There are many other miracles and stories about the power of the rosary for helping the holy souls. We need to use the rosary to free the poor souls from Purgatory. Everyone who prays rosaries should also join the *Confraternity of the Rosary* to increase the power of their prayers. We all have many family and friends who are in Purgatory that need our help. Spend 15 minutes a day with your rosary praying for them. It is a devotion that you will be greatly rewarded for doing.

Part 4

Prayers and Devotions

With Charity towards the dead we practice all the works of charity. The Church encourages us to aid the souls in purgatory, who in turn will reward us abundantly when they come into their glory.

St. Francis de Sales

Chapter 18
Catholic Mass

The center of the Catholic Church is the Mass. The Liturgy of the Eucharist is an ancient practice which goes back to the Last Supper with the first Mass. Its the main way that we worship God and petition requests to Him. This is also the most effective means to help the holy souls.

How does the Mass help the souls in Purgatory? This is the most powerful way to pray for them, followed by the Rosary. More souls are released by the Mass than any other means. St. Jerome said that *"for every Mass devoutly celebrated, many souls leave Purgatory and fly to Heaven"*. St. Bernadette, who had a great devotion for the holy souls, would tell her fellow religious sisters *"I have heard Mass for the souls in Purgatory: nothing but the Precious Blood of Jesus applied for them, can liberate them"*. St. John Vianney (the Curé d'Ars) emphasized that the Mass is greater than any works preformed, "All good works taken together cannot equal the value of one Holy Mass; because they are the works of men, whereas Holy Mass is the work of God". The Mass is the most effective way to help the holy souls in Purgatory.

We can help the holy souls by offering a Mass for them. This is involves speaking to a priest and arranging a date for the Mass. The cost in Canada for this is typically $10, but this is a free will offering and can be changed by the priest. It will also vary around the world. Poorer countries would require smaller amounts of money. I have to stress that you can't buy someone out of Purgatory. This isn't a service that the Church markets to increase its cash flow. If it was, then its a very poor way to make money. Considerably more money is made through offerings on a Sunday Mass.

Chapter 19
The Rosary

The rosary is a traditional Catholic devotion that was given to Saint Dominic in an apparition of the Blessed Virgin Mary in 1214. The word rosary is derived from *rosarium*, which is Latin for "rose garden". The purpose of this devotion is to meditate on the mysteries in the history of our salvation. It consists of three sets of mysteries which are broken up in five groups (or decades) that consist of 11 beads: 10 for Hail Mary prayers starting with an Our Father and ending with a Glory Be prayer. Its been said that a sign of a true Catholic is devotion to Mary, especially one who carries a rosary in their pocket. This is one of the great devotions in the Catholic faith and I recommend all to pray this daily.

Many people don't pray the rosary, they just say it. The correct words come out of their mouth while their minds wander. Each decade of the rosary is associated with a mystery to be meditated upon. This meditation is not the same as that used in Eastern religions where they empty their head of all thoughts. Instead, each decade is actively thought about while saying the prayer words. The three prayers in each decade is a timing mechanism which takes about three minutes to complete before moving to the next part of the rosary.

The next question is: what do you think of while praying a mystery? Most of the rosary is based directly on the Bible so its important to read and understand what is written. If you don't regularly read the Bible, this is a good reason to start.

It takes about 15 minutes to pray a mystery of the rosary. Everyone has time to pray at least one mystery a day. If not, then spend a day writing down all of your activities, including your idle times. If you don't have time for prayer your Christian life has to be seriously questioned because your putting worldly affairs ahead of God.

You don't have to pray all three mysteries of the rosary everyday. Start with one and try to increase it later. Remember that you are praying this to help the souls in Purgatory. The rosary is the most powerful prayer after the Mass and you have the advantage of being able to pray it anywhere at anytime.

How To Pray The Rosary

A great place to learn how to pray the rosary is from the group who brought it to us, the Dominican Fathers in their Rosary Center website. The instructions for the rosary can be found at https://www.rosarycenter.org/homepage-2/rosary/how-to-pray-the-rosary/. For the most benefit in praying the rosary, enroll in the Rosary Confraternity through this site. In addition to getting special protection from the Mother of God, you will also get various partial and plenary indulgences.

Fifteen Promises of Mary to Christians Who Recite the Rosary

Whoever shall faithfully serve me by the recitation of the rosary, shall receive signal graces.

1. I promise my special protection and the greatest graces to all those who shall recite the rosary.
2. The rosary shall be a powerful armor against Hell, it will destroy vice, decrease sin, and defeat heresies.
3. It will cause virtue and good works to flourish; it will obtain for souls the abundant mercy of God; it will withdraw the hearts of men from the love of the world and its vanities, and will lift them to the desire of eternal things. Oh, that souls would sanctify themselves by this means.
4. The soul which recommends itself to me by the recitation of the rosary, shall not perish.

5. Whoever shall recite the rosary devoutly, applying himself to the consideration of its sacred mysteries shall never be conquered by misfortune. God will not chastise him in His justice, he shall not perish by an unprovided death; if he but just he shall remain in the grace of God, and become worthy of eternal life.
6. Whosoever shall have a true devotion for the rosary shall not die without the sacraments of the Church.
7. Those who are faithful to recite the rosary shall have during their life and at their death the light of God and the plenitude of His graces; at the moment of death they shall participate in the merits of the saints in paradise.
8. I shall deliver from Purgatory those who have been devoted to the rosary.
9. The faithful children of the rosary shall merit a high degree of glory in Heaven.
10. You shall obtain all you ask of me by the recitation of the rosary.
11. All those who propagate the holy rosary shall be aided by me in their necessities.
12. I have obtained from my Divine Son that all the advocates of the rosary shall have for intercessors the entire celestial court during their life and at the hour of death.
13. All who recite the rosary are my sons, and brothers of my only son Jesus Christ.
14. Devotion of my rosary is a great sign of predestination.

Given to St. Dominic and Blessed Alan
Imprimatur: Patrick J. Hayes, D.D. (Archbishop of New York)

Chapter 20
Psalm 130 - De Profundis

Out of the depths I have cried unto Thee, O Lord, Lord hear my voice! Let Thine ears be attentive to the voice of my supplication. If Thou, O Lord, shalt mark our iniquities, O Lord, who can abide it? For with Thee there is mercy, and by reason of Thy law I have waited for Thee, O Lord. My soul hath hoped in the Lord.

From morning watch even unto night, let Israel hope in the Lord. For with the Lord there is mercy, and with Him is plentiful redemption. And He shall redeem Israel from all its iniquities.

V. Eternal rest grant unto them, O Lord.
R. And let perpetual light shine upon them.

Let Us Pray

O God, the Creator and Redeemer of all the faithful, grant to the souls of Thy departed servants the full remission of all their sins, that through our pious supplications they may obtain that pardon which they have always desired. Thou who livest and reignest world without end.

Amen.

Chapter 21
Prayer of St. Gertrude the Great

The following prayer will release 1000 Holy Souls from Purgatory each time it is said. It came from St. Gertrude the Great. This would be a good prayer to memorize.

> Eternal Father, I offer Thee the most Precious Blood of Thy divine Son, Jesus, in union with the masses said throughout the world today, for all the Holy Souls in Purgatory, for sinners everywhere, for sinners in the universal Church, those in my own home and within my family.
>
> Amen.

Chapter 22
Infant of Prague Prayer for Poor Souls

O Infant Jesus,

I form the belief that I shall be granted forgiveness
of sins and place it into the hands of Your most Holy Mother Mary;

I commend myself to all and every Holy Mass that is celebrated this day
and all over the globe, and I offer all this on behalf of the poor souls of purgatory.

Amen.

Chapter 23
Chaplet of the Holy Souls

This devotion is a simple and quick way to pray for the Holy Souls in Purgatory. It is prayed using traditional rosary beads.

On the large beads of the Rosary recite:

"O holy Souls draw the fire of God's love into my soul to reveal Jesus crucified in me here on earth rather than hereafter in Purgatory. Amen."

On the small beads of the Rosary recite:

"Crucified Lord Jesus, have mercy on the souls in Purgatory. Amen."

At the end of the entire prayer: (3 times)

"Glory be to the Father and to the Son and to the Holy Spirit, as it was in the beginning, is now and ever shall be. Amen."

Chapter 24
Litany of the Faithful Departed

Lord, have mercy on us,
Christ, have mercy on us

Lord, have mercy on us. Christ hear us,
Christ, graciously hear us.

God the Father of Heaven,
Have mercy on the souls of the faithful departed.

God the Son, Redeemer of the world,
Have mercy on the souls of the faithful departed.

God the Holy Ghost,
Have mercy on the souls of the faithful departed.

Holy Trinity, one God,
Have mercy on the souls of the faithful departed.

Holy Mary, Mother of God,
Pray for the souls of the faithful departed.

St. Michael,
pray for the souls of the faithful departed.

All ye angels and archangels,
pray for the souls of the faithful departed.

All ye orders of blessed spirits,
pray for the souls of the faithful departed.

St. Joseph,
pray for the souls of the faithful departed.

All ye holy patriarchs and prophets,
pray for the souls of the faithful departed.

All ye holy apostles and evangelists,
pray for the souls of the faithful departed.

All ye holy martyrs,
pray for the souls of the faithful departed.

All ye holy bishops and confessors,
pray for the souls of the faithful departed.

All ye holy doctors,
pray for the souls of the faithful departed.

All ye holy priests and Levites,
pray for the souls of the faithful departed.

All ye holy monks and hermits,
pray for the souls of the faithful departed.

All ye holy virgins and widows,
pray for the souls of the faithful departed.

All ye saints of God,
pray for the souls of the faithful departed.

Be merciful,
Spare them, O Lord

Be merciful,
Graciously hear us, O Lord.

From all evil,
O Lord, deliver them.

From the rigor of Thy justice,
O Lord, deliver them.

From the power of the devil,
O Lord, deliver them.

From long-enduring sorrow,
O Lord, deliver them.

From cruel flames,
O Lord, deliver them.

From horrible darkness,
O Lord, deliver them.

From dreadful weeping and wailing,
O Lord, deliver them.

Through Thy holy nativity,
O Lord, deliver them.

Through Thy most sweet name,
O Lord, deliver them.

Through Thy most profound humiliations,
O Lord, deliver them.

Through Thy infinite love,
O Lord, deliver them.

Through Thy bloody sweat,
O Lord, deliver them.

Through Thy scourging,
O Lord, deliver them.

Through Thy crowning with thorns,
O Lord, deliver them.

Through Thy carrying of the cross,
O Lord, deliver them.

Through Thy most cruel death,
O Lord, deliver them.

Through Thy five most holy wounds,
O Lord, deliver them.

In the day of judgment,
We sinners, beseech Thee, hear us.

Thou Who forgavest Magdalen, and didst grant the prayer of the thief,
we beseech Thee, hear us.

That Thou wouldst be pleased to deliver the souls of our parents, relations, friends, and benefactors, from the pains of hell,
we beseech Thee, hear us.

That Thou wouldst be pleased to have mercy on those of whom no special remembrance
is made on earth,
we beseech Thee, hear us.

That Thou wouldst be pleased to grant them all the pardon and remission of their sins,
we beseech Thee, hear us.

That Thou wouldst be pleased to receive them into the company of the blessed,
we beseech Thee, hear us.

King of awful majesty,
we beseech Thee, hear us.

Son of God, we beseech Thee,
hear us.

Lamb of God, who takest away the sins of the world,
grant unto them eternal rest.

Lamb of God, who takest away the sins of the world,
grant unto them eternal rest.

Lamb of God, who takest away the sins of the world,
grant unto them rest everlasting.

Christ, hear us.
Christ, graciously hear us.

Lord, have mercy,
Christ, have mercy.

Lord, have mercy,
From the gate of hell,
deliver their souls, O Lord.

O Lord, hear my prayer.
And let my cry come unto Thee.

LET US PRAY:

O God, the Creator and Redeemer of all the faithful, grant unto the souls of Thy servants departed the remission of all their sins; that, by pious supplications, they may obtain the pardon which they have always desired. Grant this, O God, Who livest and reignest for ever and ever,

Amen.

O eternal God, Who, besides the general precept of charity, hast commanded a particular respect for parents, kindred, and benefactors; grant, we beseech Thee, that, as they were the instruments by which Thy providence bestowed on us our birth, education and innumerable other blessings, so our prayers may be the means to obtain for them a speedy release from their excessive sufferings, and admittance to Thine infinite joys. Through Jesus Christ, Our Lord.

Eternal rest give unto them, O Lord, And let the perpetual light shine upon them.

May they rest in peace.

Amen.

Chapter 25

Prayer to God the Father

Eternal Father, I offer Thee the Precious Blood of Jesus Christ in satisfaction for my sins, in supplication for the Holy Souls in Purgatory and for the needs of the Holy Church.

Amen.

Chapter 26
Special Offering of the Mass for the Souls in Purgatory

O God of love, Father of Our Lord Jesus Christ, on this altar behold the unbloody sacrifice of the body and blood of Thy Son, representing that of His most holy death and grievous Passion, which He, the great High Priest, offered Thee on Calvary. In consideration of this holocaust of sweet odor, have mercy on the souls in purgatory; open to them the gates of heaven, that they may love and praise Thee, and enjoy Thee eternally in the abode of the saints. Together with the sufferings of The divine Son, I likewise offer The the sorrows of His blessed mother, whose souls was crucified at the foot of her Son's cross; for the lance which pierced the side and heart of Jesus, thine adorable Son, also transfixed the soul and heart of Mary, according to Simeon's prophecy, and made her the queen of martyrs. Behold then , O heavenly Father! the disfigured countenance of They Son on the cross and the crucified heart of His Mother at the foot of this same cross; and by the merits of all the sufferings of that son and that Mother, grant eternal repose to the souls in purgatory.

Saint Alphonsus Liguori

Chapter 27
The Chaplet of St. Michael

Saint Michael appearing one day to Antonia d'Astonac, a most devout Servant of God, told her that he wished to be honoured by nine salutations corresponding to the nine Choirs of Angels, which should consist of one Our Father and three Hail Marys in honour of each of the angelic choirs.

Promises of St. Michael

Whosoever would practice this devotion in his honour would have, when approaching the Holy Table, an escort of nine angels chosen from each one of the nine choirs. In addition, for the daily recital of these nine salutations he promised his continual assistance and that of all the holy angels during life, and after death deliverance from Purgatory for themselves and their relations.

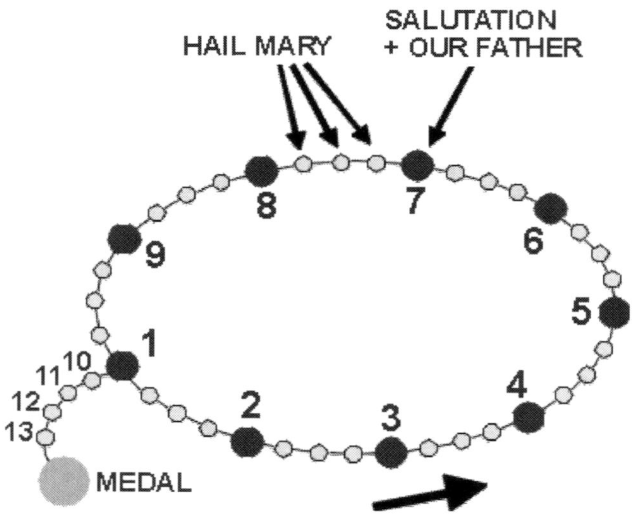

Method of Reciting the Chaplet

There are nine beads plus a medal on the chaplet. You begin by saying the following invocation on the medal.

MEDAL

O God, come to my assistance.
O Lord, make haste to help me.
Glory Be

FIRST BEAD

By the intercession of St. Michael and celestial Choir of Seraphim, may the Lord make us worthy to burn with the fire of perfect charity.

Our Father, then 3 Hail Marys

Amen.

SECOND BEAD

By the intercession of St. Michael and the celestial Choir of Cherubim, may the Lord vouchsafe to grant us grace to leave the ways of wickedness to run in the paths of Christian perfection.

Our Father, then 3 Hail Marys

Amen.

THIRD BEAD

By the intercession of St. Michael and the celestial Choir of Thrones, may the Lord infuse into our hearts a true and sincere spirit of humility.

Our Father, then 3 Hail Marys

Amen.

FOURTH BEAD

By the intercession of St. Michael and the celestial Choice of Dominions, may the Lord give us grace to govern our senses and subdue our unruly passions.

Our Father, then 3 Hail Marys

Amen.

FIFTH BEAD

By the intercession of St. Michael and the celestial Choir of Powers, may the Lord vouchsafe to protect our souls against the snares and temptations of the devil.

Our Father, then 3 Hail Marys

Amen.

SIXTH BEAD

By the intercession of St. Michael and the celestial Choir of Virtues, may the Lord preserve us from evil and suffer us not to fall into temptation.

Our Father, then 3 Hail Marys

Amen.

SEVENTH BEAD

By the intercession of St. Michael and the celestial Choir of Principalities, may God fill our souls with a true spirit of obedience.

Our Father, then 3 Hail Marys

Amen.

EIGHTH BEAD

By the intercession of St. Michael and the celestial Choir of Archangel, may the Lord give us perseverance in faith and in all good works, in order that we gain the glory of Paradise.

Our Father, then 3 Hail Marys

Amen.

NINTH BEAD

By the intercession of St. Michael and the celestial Choir of Angels, may the Lord grant us to be protected by them in this mortal life and conducted hereafter to eternal glory.

Our Father, then 3 Hail Marys

Amen.

On the 4 remaining beads, say one Our Father in honour of each of the following angels: St. Michael, St. Gabriel, St. Raphael, and our Guardian Angel.

The chaplet is concluded with the following prayers:

V. Pray for us, O glorious St. Michael, Prince of the Church of Jesus Christ
R. That we may be made worthy of His promises.

Almighty and Everlasting God, who by a prodigy of goodness and a merciful desire for the salvation of all men, hast appointed the most glorious Archangel, St. Michael, Prince of Thy Church, make us worthy, we beseech Thee, to be delivered from all our enemies that none of them may harass us at the hour of death, but that we may conducted by him into the august presence of Thy Divine Majesty. This we beg through the merits of Jesus Christ our Lord.

Amen.

(With Ecclesiastical Approval)

Chapter 28
The Flame of Love

Between the years 1961 and 1981 in Hungary, Elizabeth Kindelmann received apparitions and messages from the Lord Jesus and the Virgin Mary. The central theme was the Flame of Love of Mary's Immaculate Heart. Jesus revealed to Elizabeth that "*the Flame of Love of my Mother is for you what the ark was for Noah*". Our Blessed Mother then added, "*the Flame of Love of my Immaculate Heart is Jesus Christ Himself!*"

What does the Flame of Love have to do with Purgatory? On October 13, 1962 (the 45th anniversary of the final apparition at Fatima), Our Lady revealed to Elizabeth the following message:

"*My Daughter, your compassion for suffering souls moved my Motherly heart so much that I will grant the grace that if anyone anywhere will say Three Hail Mary's in reference to my Flame of Love, then on each occasion a soul will be freed from Purgatory. Furthermore, "In the month of the Holy Souls [November] ten souls will be freed from Purgatory for each Hail Mary ... Suffering souls will also feel the effect of the grace coming from my Motherly Flame of Love.*"

This is a simple devotion that can be said frequently to help the souls in Purgatory. Our Lady also revealed a way to help family members suffering in Purgatory:

"Families doing the hour of atonement on Thursdays or Fridays will receive the special grace of delivering from Purgatory, within eight days, one deceased member of their family after one single day of severe fasting [on water and bread]."

While the Flame of Love is not focused on devotions to Purgatory, there are many references in on how we can help the holy souls. You can learn more by visiting https://www.theflameoflove.org/.

Chapter 29
The Rosary of the Holy Wounds

> *"When you offer My Holy Wounds for sinners, you must not forget to do so for the souls in Purgatory, as there are but few who think of their relief. . . The Holy wounds are the treasure of treasures for the souls in Purgatory."*
>
> Our Lord, according to Sr. Mary Martha Chambon

There are many uses of rosary beads. The greatest of course is the Marian rosary, but there have been many other devotions that use these beads. One of them is the Rosary of the Holy Wounds. It has been given to us by Jesus, according to Sister Mary Martha Chambon (1841-1907). She was a nun at the Monastery of the Visitation of Chambery in France. The cause for her canonization as a saint began in 1937.

Jesus made many promises to those who would honor His Holy Wounds by praying this rosary. Some of them are:

- At each word that you pronounce of the Chaplet of the Holy Wounds, I allow a drop of My Blood to fall upon the soul of a sinner.
- I will grant all that is asked of Me through the invocation of My Holy Wounds. You will obtain everything, because it is through the merit of My Blood, which is of infinite price. With My Wounds and My Divine Heart, everything can be obtained

- My Wounds will repair yours. My Wounds will cover all your faults. Those who honor them will have a true knowledge of Jesus Christ. In meditation on them, you will always find a new love. My wounds will cover all your sins.
- When you have some trouble, something to suffer, quickly place it in My Wounds, and the pain will be alleviated.
- There will be no death for the soul that expires in My Holy Wounds; they give true life.
- Those who pray with humility and who meditate on My Passion, will one day participate in the glory of My divine Wounds.
- The soul who during life has honoured the Wounds of our Lord Jesus Christ and has offered them to the Eternal Father for the Souls in Purgatory, will be accompanied at the moment of death by the Holy Virgin and the angels; and Our Lord on the Cross, all brilliant in glory, will receive her and crown her.

Our Lord also made a promise to St. Gertrude for those who honour His Holy Wounds. She had a vision of Jesus after finishing her prayers for His wounds at one time. There were golden roses on top of His wounds. Jesus then said, "*Behold, I will appear to you in this radiant form at the hour of your death, and I will cover all your sins, and adorn you with a glory like that with which you have adorned My Wounds by your salutations. All who do so shall receive the like favour.*"

The method of praying this rosary is as follows. You begin with,

> O Jesus, Divine Redeemer, be merciful to us and to the whole world. Amen.

> Strong God, Holy God, Immortal God, have mercy on us and on the whole world. Amen.
>
> Grace and Mercy, O my Jesus, during present dangers; cover us with Your Precious Blood. Amen.
>
> Eternal Father, grant us mercy through the Blood of Jesus Christ, Your only Son; grant us mercy we beseech You. Amen.

On the "Our Father" beads (the larger ones) you pray,

> Eternal Father, I offer You the Wounds of Our Lord, Jesus Christ, to heal the wounds of our souls.

And on the smaller "Hail Mary" beads you pray,

> My Jesus, pardon and mercy, through the merits of Your Holy Wounds.

At the very end of the rosary, at the "Hail, Holy Queen" part, conclude by praying the following three times,

> Eternal Father, I offer You the Wounds of Our Lord, Jesus Christ, to heal the wounds of our souls.

Chapter 30
The Seven Our Fathers and Hail Marys

In a private revelation to Saint Bridget, Our Lord revealed a devotion to honour His Holy Wounds and Precious Blood. It was a daily recital of seven Our Fathers and seven Hail Marys for twelve years:

"Know that I will grant the following five graces to those who recite every day for twelve years (or until their death, should they die before):

1. *They will avoid Purgatory.*
2. *They will be numbered amongst the martyrs, as though they had shed their blood for the faith.*
3. *I will maintain the souls of three of their children (or relatives) in a state of sanctifying grace.*
4. *The souls of their relatives, up to four generations, will avoid Hell.*
5. *They will know the date of their death one month in advance."*

This revelation was confirmed by Pope Innocent X who added that a soul will be released from Purgatory on Good Fridays through this devotion.

Part 5

Appendix

If you deliver one soul from Purgatory, you can say with confidence, "Heaven is mine".

St. Leonard

Chapter 31
Where To Go From Here

Now that your full of knowledge of what Purgatory is and how to help the holy souls there, where do you go from here? This book, as its title implies, is an introduction to Purgatory, a first course. It's by no means the final word on the subject as there is still much to learn after this.

There are many books and other resources where you can discover more about Purgatory. While its important to learn more, you have to keep in mind the main purpose of studying this topic: **you want to help free the holy souls from Purgatory so they can enter Heaven.** The key to success here is a consistent devotion. Choose something that you can do regularly and every day if possible.

The holy soul that you pray for may not have anyone else helping them. Your sacrifices and devotions are more important than you can imagine. Use your newly acquired knowledge to help your suffering brothers and sisters and encourage others to do the same.

Chapter 32
Further Reading

> "To be ignorant of Scripture is to be ignorant of Christ."
>
> St. Jerome

The following is a list of sources for you to grow in knowledge in Purgatory.

1. The Bible

Every Catholic should read the Bible every day, but sadly, most do not. If you want a true devotion to the souls in Purgatory and if you want to have a positive effect influencing others in this devotion, you need to read and understand the Bible, in particular the Gospels. Frank Sheed (a famous street corner apologist from the 20th Century) said that "*a Catholic apologist who is not soaked in the Gospels is an anomaly in himself, and his work is doomed to aridity*".

2. Catholicism and Fundamentalism

If your promoting devotion to the holy souls, you will very likely be engaged in debates with unbelievers on Catholic doctrines. Most Catholics know very little of their faith and wouldn't know how to explain Catholicism when cornered.

Karl Keating's book, Catholicism and Fundamentalism, not only defines the major Catholic doctrines, but gives reasons why they should be believed. This is the role of an apologist: explaining and defending their faith. When I converted away from Protestant

Fundamentalism, this book was instrumental in showing me that Catholicism was true and was founded by Jesus Christ. If you don't understand your faith and can't explain your beliefs, this book will show you Catholicism and answer your questions.

Karl Keating is the president of Catholic Answers (www.catholic.com), which is a great source of apologetics information.

3. Read Me or Rue It; How To Avoid Purgatory

This classical work will inspire you and touch your heart with a devotion to the holy souls. This is the first book I read on Purgatory, and I read it as a Protestant. It had such a great effect on me that years later I created a web site to promote devotion to the holy souls. This book can be purchased at most Catholic stores, or you can read it for free on http://www.ecclesiabytes.com.

4. Susan Tassone

Like Keating, Tassone is a lay person promoting Catholicism. She is an advocate of the holy souls and has written many inspirational and spiritual books on helping them. Susan can be found online at http://susantassone.com.

5. Ecclesia Bytes Website and Podcast

I started a web site to promote the doctrine of Purgatory in 1998 (Holy Souls Online) on the now shut down GeoCities. This one was one of my first web sites and it was built when free hosting was very appealing that time. It was an extensive resource on articles on Purgatory, devotions, and forums to ask questions or discuss ideas. The site evolved from static HTML pages on

GeoCities, to hosting as a subdomain on one of my business sites, to self-hosted on www.holysouls.info, a domain name change to www.holysoulsonline.com, and finally it because a part of http://www.ecclesiabytes.com. The new site has the content of the Holy Souls Online, a free e-book download of this book (Purgatory 101), and the Ecclesia Bytes Catholic Podcast.

Printed in Great Britain
by Amazon

47732650R00059